DAY OF THE DEAD

By

Shalini Vallepur

BookLife
PUBLISHING

©2021
BookLife Publishing Ltd.
King's Lynn
Norfolk, PE30 4LS

All rights reserved.
Printed in Malta.

A catalogue record for
this book is available from
the British Library.

ISBN: 978-1-83927-472-5

Written by:
Shalini Vallepur

Edited by:
Madeline Tyler

Designed by:
Drue Rintoul

Photo Credits
All images are courtesy of Shutterstock.com. With thanks to Getty Images, Thinkstock Photo and iStockphoto. Front Cover – Leon Rafael. 2–3 – Fer Gregory. 4–5 – bmszealand, Leon Rafael, Roberto Michel. 6–7 – matias planas, Quetzalcoatl1. 8–9 – Prokhorovich. 10–11 – erd_1981. 12–13 – Carlos Ivan Palacios, AGCuesta. 14–15 – Kobby Dagan, AGCuesta. 16–17 – Kobby Dagan, Roberto Michel. 18–19 – Quetzalcoatl1. 20–21 – Suriel Ramzal, William Neuheisel / CC BY. 22–23 – ShengYing Lin, Leon Rafael, BestStockFoto.

CONTENTS

Words that look like <u>this</u> can be found in the glossary on page 24.

CELEBRATE DAY OF THE DEAD WITH ME!

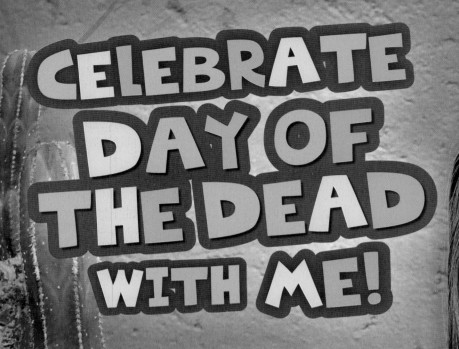

My name is Rosa. I'm here to tell you about the Day of the Dead! Day of the Dead is a time for families, friends and the <u>community</u> to come together.

Day of the Dead is called Día de los Muertos in Spanish.

We remember and <u>honour</u> those who have passed away. We do this through playing music, eating food and laughter.

We try not to be sad during Day of the Dead.

DAY OF THE DEAD

We celebrate Day of the Dead over two days – November 1st and 2nd. At midnight on the first day, we celebrate Día de los Angelitos. This is when children who have passed away are remembered.

Día de los Angelitos means Day of the Little Angels.

Día de los Difuntos starts at midnight on the second day. We celebrate the adults who have passed away. We spend the night laughing and remembering fun memories.

Día de los Difuntos also means Day of the Dead.

THE HISTORY OF DAY OF THE DEAD

Hundreds of years ago in what is now Mexico, the Nahua people, including the Aztecs, celebrated a festival like Day of the Dead. They believed that when a person died, their <u>spirit</u> went on a hard journey to a place called Mictlán. Mictlán was ruled by different gods and goddesses.

The Nahua people would try to please the gods in Mictlán with a festival that lasted a month. They would make <u>offerings</u> to the gods. They would also bury people who died with lots of offerings and gifts. They believed that the offerings would help the spirits find their way to Mictlán.

Over time, the dates of this festival changed and it became a two-day festival. Although some things changed, many of the <u>traditions</u> are the same.

During Day of the Dead, we believe that the spirits of the dead come back to our world. We believe that they come to visit their families so we offer them food and drink. We also try not to be very sad. We remember that death is a part of life and we try to be happy and remember the people who have left us.

ALTARS

Altars are made before Day of the Dead celebrations begin. They are made in our homes and in <u>cemeteries</u> near the grave of the person who has died. We also clean the grave.

Altar at night

The Spanish word for altar is ofrenda.

Altars and graves are decorated with flowers called Mexican marigolds. We believe the bright flowers help the spirits of the dead to find their way to their altar.

Can you see the Mexican marigolds?

VISITING CEMETERIES

On Day of the Dead, we put offerings on the altars. These are usually things that the person liked when they were alive.

Offerings could be family photos and their favourite snacks, drinks or toys.

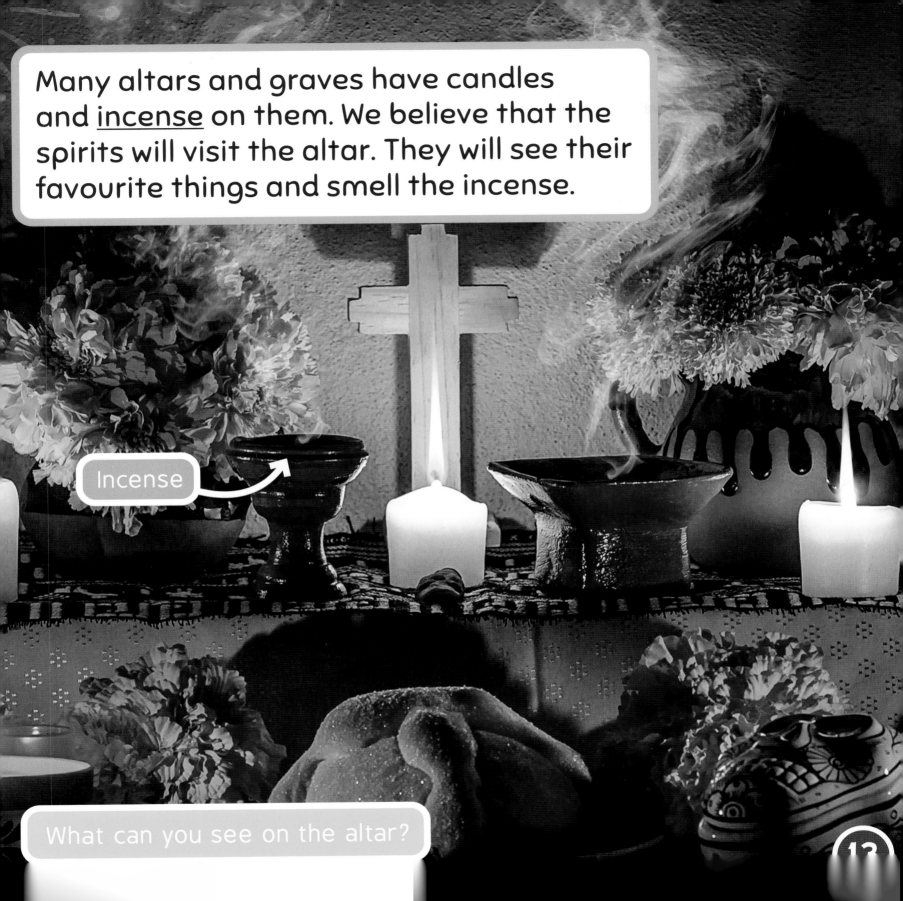

Many altars and graves have candles and <u>incense</u> on them. We believe that the spirits will visit the altar. They will see their favourite things and smell the incense.

Incense

What can you see on the altar?

SKULLS

We put things that look like skulls on the altar. This is very important because they remind us that we are not here forever.

The word calavera means skull in Spanish.

Skulls made from sugar are put on the altars too.
We decorate them with bright colours. Sometimes we
write the name of the person who has passed away on it.

Sugar skull

MARIACHI AND PRAYERS

Mariachi bands come to the cemeteries at night. They play music for both the living and the spirits of the dead to enjoy. Some people will ask the bands to play songs that the dead liked.

Say: ma-ree-aa-chee

Mariachi band

16

Some people say prayers when they arrive at the cemetery. In some parts of Mexico, people light lots of candles in the cemetery. This is called La Alumbrada.

PARADES

Some cities and towns have <u>parades</u> or street parties for Day of the Dead. There are big <u>floats</u> with mariachi bands and dancers.

It is very colourful!

Many people wear costumes and paint skulls on their faces. Some people dress up as skeletons. It is a time for using music and dancing to remember the dead.

FESTIVE FOOD

Delicious food is eaten throughout Day of the Dead. Bread of the dead is sugary and delicious. Most people put a loaf of it on their altars along with sugar skulls.

Bread of the dead is called pan de muerto in Spanish.

We eat mole negro during Day of the Dead too. It is a sauce made from peppers, chocolate and many other things. It can take a long time to make so it is very special.

Mole negro

Some people leave their dead loved one's favourite meal as an offering on the altar.

DAY OF THE DEAD AROUND THE WORLD

Day of the Dead is mainly celebrated in Mexico, but there are many celebrations around the world.

This celebration is in the US, where Day of the Dead is becoming a popular festival.

Thank you for learning about Day of the Dead with me! I hope you understand why and how we celebrate it. Why not check if there is a Day of the Dead parade in your area?

23

GLOSSARY

altars	tables that are used to make offerings
cemeteries	places where people are buried when they die
community	a group of people who are connected by something
floats	small platforms on a moving cart or car used in processions
honour	when people remember and respect something
incense	a material that makes a nice smell when burned
mariachi	a type of Mexican music performed by a small group of musicians
offerings	things that are given away as part of worship
parades	when people walk or dance down a street with people watching
spirit	the part of a person that is believed to live forever
traditions	beliefs and actions that are passed down between people over time

INDEX